The invisible child

The
invisible
child

The responses and attitudes to the learning of modern foreign languages shown by Year 9 pupils of average ability

A report of a joint research project carried out by CILT and Barking and Dagenham LEA

Jeff Lee, David Buckland and Glenis Shaw

CiLT
Centre for Information
on Language Teaching and Research

The views expressed in this publication are the authors' and do not necessarily represent those of CILT.

First published in 1998
Copyright © 1998
Centre for Information on Language Teaching and Research
ISBN 1 874016 96 8
A catalogue record for this book is available from the British Library

Printed in Great Britain by Copyprint (UK) Ltd
Cover design by Marc Padellec

Published by the Centre for Information on Language Teaching and Research,
20 Bedfordbury, Covent Garden, London WC2N 4LB.

CILT Publications are available from: **Central Books,** 99 Wallis Rd, London
E9 5LN. Tel: 0845 458 9910. Fax: 0845 458 9912. Book trade representation
(UK and Ireland): **Broadcast Book Services,** Charter House, 27a London
Road, Croydon CR0 2RE. Tel: 020 8681 8949. Fax: 020 8688 0615.

Contents

Acknowledgements

The project team would like to thank the 62 Year 9 pupils of Barking and Dagenham who took part in this research. Their informative and often very perceptive responses made the fieldwork enjoyable and productive for the interviewers and made it possible for some very important messages to be learned.

The research team is also extremely grateful to staff in the following Barking and Dagenham schools:

- All Saints RC Comprehensive School
- Barking Abbey Comprehensive School
- Dagenham Priory Comprehensive School
- Eastbrook Comprehensive School
- Eastbury Comprehensive School
- Robert Clack Comprehensive School
- Sydney Russell Comprehensive School
- Warren Comprehensive School

Without the full co-operation and support of head teachers and modern languages staff in these schools this project could not have been carried out. Thanks are also due to the staff and pupils of Sheredes School, Hoddesdon, for their invaluable help with the trialling of the interview questions.

The authors would also like to thank Ros Mitchell for her helpful comments on an earlier draft of the text.

Preface

Lid King, Director, CILT

———————— ◀▶ ————————

The National Curriculum's introduction of foreign language learning for all pupils in secondary education has been a major achievement. As with any achievement it has not been without problems. Issues such as relevance — the ways in which we devise appropriate language programmes for such a wide range of learners, progression — or the description of how those learners learn — and motivation, especially among some of the older pupils, have continued to concern teachers as well as those, such as CILT, who would help them in their work.

These, and other challenges of 'languages for all', provide a rich agenda for the end of the century. It is an agenda which involves a number of players — local and national government, agencies, advisers and teachers. Above all, if it is to be a fruitful process, it must involve the learners who are, after all, the main point of the whole exercise. It is for this reason that CILT was delighted to be able to collaborate with Barking and Dagenham LEA in a project whose aim was to talk, and in particular listen to those learners. As is explained in detail by those who took part in the project we deliberately chose to speak not to the obvious stars or failures of the education system but to those who pass through it, apparently untouched and unseen. That their views are so interesting, sometimes contradictory, often highly perceptive suggests that they are in fact much more committed to and affected by the learning process than we might think. It also sends a very positive message about the importance of education and about the very real possibilities for change.

The invisible child

Introduction

Roger Luxton, Principal Inspector,
London Borough of Barking and Dagenham

———————— ◀▶ ————————

This fascinating and original study of the attitudes and experiences of boys and girls in the field of modern foreign language learning concentrates on those Year 9 pupils of average ability who can too often become invisible, in the word of the report. They are undemanding of their teachers' time and attention and do not achieve highly. But they represent the great majority of all students. Surely, this report argues, it is important to find out the attitudes and views of this numerically dominant group — to make audible the judgements and beliefs of the invisible. They have been listened to at length and with great care.

Their voices speak out loud and clear. There is much to encourage teachers of modern languages. In the past the received wisdom has been that boys and girls of average or below average ability simply don't want to go on learning modern foreign languages; they can't see the point in a world apparently dominated by English. When, and if, they go abroad, they find it much easier to converse in English. Boys are held to be even less interested than girls.

A careful reading of this report, which contains an abundance of information and insights, challenges this received wisdom. These boys and girls do think it is important to learn a foreign language. They have a view as to why it is important. They describe the way they conceive of their own strengths and weaknesses. In Year 9 nearly three-quarters of them claim to be as positive about language learning as when they started, or more so. This is far from being a bleak picture.

However, there are some other important messages. These pupils lack a clear view of what learning a language really means. They are unclear about what they are supposed to gain from their lessons. The report offers a number of pointers to addressing these problems, to building upon and strengthening the pupils' motivation in future, in order to enhance their attainment, progress and enjoyment in learning. These lessons should be absorbed and used to improve practice.

This report deserves to have a considerable impact on the teaching of modern foreign languages. I should like to thank David Buckland, Glenis Shaw and Jeff Lee for their skilful work in obtaining so much valuable information and for presenting it in such an accessible form. I should also like to thank CILT for their invaluable co-operation. Barking and Dagenham LEA is very pleased to have made its contribution to the question of understanding pupil motivation in the field of modern language learning.

Section

1 ▶ Introduction and background

This report sets out the findings of a research project set up to investigate pupil motivation in the field of modern foreign language learning. The field work was carried out during May and June 1997. The project arose from an approach made by CILT to the modern languages inspection and advisory team at Barking and Dagenham LEA; both bodies had worked together previously and had shared their expertise on developments in teaching support and pupil attainment in modern languages.

The impetus for the project stemmed from a common concern to investigate the responses of average pupils in Year 9 to mainstream modern language learning, as a guide to identifying factors affecting levels of motivation. Not all elements or initiatives in education are given similar or equal attention. The project focuses quite deliberately on a moderately large group of pupils, from eight comprehensive schools, whose nature means they are rarely the subject of special interest.

Barking and Dagenham as an area was for many years largely 'invisible' in the education world. It received little or no attention through publicity and the media and little by way of special resources. It demonstrated no outstanding social problems or exceptional characteristics. It is a working-class suburb of East London where socio-economic conditions have been stable for many years and where there has been relatively little population movement or demographic change. The OFSTED report *Access and achievement in urban education* (HMSO, 1993) describes educational provision and attainment in a number of areas which closely resemble Barking and

5

Dagenham. Educational standards in the borough were for a long time consistently among the lowest nationally, though recently there has been a significant improvement. Schools in this LEA have been identified since the early 1990s as among the fastest improving in the country.

Children too can be 'invisible': many are undemanding in terms of attention and inconspicuous in terms of achievement. An invisible child for the purpose of this research is defined as one who is unexceptional in identifiable characteristics such as attainment, ability, learning behaviour, attendance and social behaviour. An invisible child does not demand or attract special attention or consideration from the teacher, apparently working conscientiously and, in the main, achieving standards of attainment which are not noticeably high or low. Teachers rarely mention such pupils, yet they are perhaps representative of many. For these pupils, as indeed for all, Year 9 is crucial.

Although standards of attainment in modern languages have risen appreciably in Barking and Dagenham over recent years, the number of pupils achieving the middle- and lower-order GCSE grades has tended to remained stubbornly high. It is argued that if the key can be found to helping such average pupils to raise their standards, without diminishing the performance of the more able, the average level of attainment will itself by definition rise. Discussions with teachers have suggested that levels of motivation, especially in Year 9 and above, may be a key factor. The reasons for any such low motivation and levels of self-perception need to be understood before any remedial action can be taken.

It is not automatically the case that children of average ability, and who do not draw attention to themselves in other ways, will receive less direct attention than pupils who readily achieve a high standard of work, or have obvious learning difficulties, or possess more assertive personalities. However, many who have taught a wide range of pupils would say that on balance such 'average' pupils get a less than average share of attention. The research team readily accepts that some might set out to disprove this but argues that it is permissible to proceed on this basis. It can be argued that the majority of children are not by nature especially high or low attainers, and the OFSTED report *Access and achievement in urban education* refers to '. . . the few who were reluctant learners . . .' and '. . . the many who were co-operative'. In other words, most accept the work they are given, do their best without complaint, and are not badly behaved. In any case, it is perhaps less important to determine the quantity of direct teacher attention given to pupils than it is to observe the nature, and impact on motivation, of the overall provision which pupils actually receive, whether direct or not.

In initial planning discussions between CILT and the LEA, three starting points were identified:

- a concern with levels of achievement in modern languages of averagely attaining children and the role played here by motivation or lack of it;

- an interest in investigating why many of these pupils in Key Stage 3 appear to lack motivation to learn a modern language;

- an interest in establishing, on the basis of what they say about modern language learning and in the light of existing knowledge about motivation in education, how the motivation of these pupils can best be improved.

The second of these was based to some extent on an assumption, anecdotal and impressionistic, and without reference to the distinction between the different aspects of motivation or factors affecting it. It subsequently became clear through the research interviews that pupils distinguished in their own way quite clearly between these different aspects and were not in general negatively disposed towards modern languages. The analysis of pupils' responses gradually built up a more complex picture of the associated problems than was originally expected.

At a more detailed level, the interview questions aimed to determine pupils' perceptions and experience of their modern language learning, including enjoyment levels, their views on the nature and process of language learning, their views on achievement and progress (personal and general), accounts of how they obtained help and support and how they organised their learning, and their perceptions of the status and importance of foreign language learning. Analysis of their responses would help to inform planning and recommendations for ways of improving achievement in modern languages.

This report sets out the pupils' responses and seeks to analyse them and establish some conclusions which it is hoped will be helpful for teachers and others concerned with modern language provision.

Section

2

Profile of the pupils

The Borough has eight 11–18 all-ability mixed secondary schools. Each school was asked to identify eight pupils for interview. Schools were asked to select four boys and four girls who:

- were in the 1996/97 Year 9 cohort (i.e. pupils who would shortly be assessed on their standards and progress in National Curriculum/level description terms);

- had been learning French or German in their Barking and Dagenham school since Year 7;

- were of average ability, i.e. likely to attain GCSE grade D or E, and currently in a mid-ability set (if ability grouping used);

- were 'invisible', as defined in Section 1 of this report: unexceptional in terms of attainment, ability, and behaviour;

- were in two different teaching groups.

These criteria were accepted by all the schools as clear and workable for the purpose of this research, and in general suitable pupils could be readily identified. In one school only six pupils were available on the day, resulting in a total of 62 pupils (31 boys and 31 girls) being interviewed across the LEA. This represents 3.4% of the Borough's total Year 9 population (in the academic year 1996/97) of 1825 pupils. Of the 62 pupils, 54 were studying French and eight German as their first foreign language. Four of those studying French were learning Russian as a second foreign language.

Barking and Dagenham is predominantly a white working-class area. While the selection of the sample did not formally include ethnicity as a selection criterion, teachers in schools with a significant minority ethnic population were asked to include pupils from a range of backgrounds. Further information about the pupils' backgrounds, and links with foreign cultures and languages, emerged during the interviews. This occurred when pupils' views on learning a modern language were sought and when they were asked what their parents thought about their learning a language (Questions 21 and 22).

The 62 pupils interviewed included:

- one girl from Colombia, Spanish native speaker, four years in England, cousin living in France;

- one girl with Afro-Caribbean family background;

- one boy with Tunisian family background;

- two girls who are native speakers of Urdu;

- one boy who is a native speaker of Urdu;

- one boy who is a native speaker of Gujerati;

- one Turkish boy.

In addition, five pupils mentioned a relative working in a job with foreign language aspects; three mentioned family links with other countries (e.g. mother half-Italian).

Section

3

Research method and the interview questions

Research method

In order to gain as full an understanding as possible of the pupils' perceptions of and responses to their modern language learning, the study was detailed and in-depth; data produced was largely qualitative rather than quantitative. The most reliable format was judged to be a small-scale study involving open-ended questions, administered in face-to-face interviews with the pupils.

The LEA's schools were introduced to the project during 1996/97. It was essential to ensure the full support of senior management and the co-operation of modern language teachers, though this needed to be balanced against the risk of raising the public profile of the work to an unnecessary level. The intention was for the project to be small-scale and provisional in nature, with low-profile informal feedback offered to departments immediately after their pupils were interviewed.

Two potential problems were identified:

- the danger of schools, and especially modern language teachers, perceiving the project as yet another inspection of their work, albeit an indirect one;

- pupils' responses to the interviews being distorted or influenced in any way by inappropriate prior knowledge or perceptions.

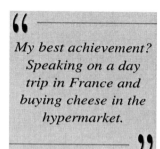

My best achievement? Speaking on a day trip in France and buying cheese in the hypermarket.

In practice no evidence of these problems occurring was apparent to the project team, although there is always the risk that the mere fact of being interviewed in this way can affect responses.

Oral briefings were given to head teachers and modern languages staff about the background, objectives, nature and intended outcomes of the project. Written guidance was sent to heads of department about working procedures, practical arrangements and the offer of feedback to the department after the pupil interviews. In addition heads of department were supplied with the text of an explanatory letter to be sent to parents of pupils involved. Teachers were asked to give brief information to pupils and to reassure them that the interviews would not form any kind of test but would be important in the work of supporting language teaching.

Pupils were interviewed in pairs. The text of the questions (see Appendix) shows where individual responses were sought and where the two pupils could confer. One interviewer led the questioning while the other took notes. Each interview lasted approximately 45 minutes and was tape-recorded. At each school the interviewers met all the pupils together for ten minutes before the interviews to outline what would be happening and deal with any questions the pupils had about the procedures.

The interview questions

The interview questions were trialled in schools outside the LEA. They are grouped under five main headings for the purpose of subsequent analysis (the examples are indicative of the type of questions asked rather than exact wordings used). The first four groups (A–D, Questions 1–20) deal with pupils' responses to their experiences of language learning and are designed to explore aspects of pupils' intrinsic motivation: their interest in the subject, their feelings about the progress they are making, etc. Group E (Questions 21–25) deals more with pupils' views of the importance of language learning generally and to them, i.e. with aspects of extrinsic motivation.

A (qq 1–2): preference (across a range of subjects). Examples: put these subjects in order of preference/why do you prefer your first choice?

B (qq 3–11): modern language lessons. Examples: what kind of things do you do in your modern language lessons?/were you clear what you were supposed to learn from your last lesson?

C (qq 12–18): language learning. Examples: what do you need in order to learn a language well?/what sort of problems do you come across when you are trying to learn?

D (qq 19–20): progress. Examples: do you think the standard of your work is getting higher? If so, in what ways?

E (qq 21–25): attitudes. Examples: is it important to learn a foreign language?/do you feel differently about language learning now compared to when you started in Year 7?

The five section headings were not given to pupils. The questions were not designed or worded either explicitly or implicitly to relate specifically to aspects of the National Curriculum in modern languages, or to additional provision such as visits abroad; rather they were designed to enable pupils to recognise and talk about routine classroom experiences in everyday terms. The questions are set out in full in the Appendix, with any notes about how the responses were to be given and noted, and are also included in Section 4: the pupils' responses.

In retrospect, greater emphasis could have been given, in question groups B and C, to the role of memorising as an explicit process within language learning, whether as a lesson activity or as a problem experienced while learning.

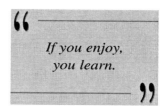

If you enjoy, you learn.

Analysis of responses

The pupils' responses were analysed manually by the project team. The interviewers' notes were the main source of information, with the tape recordings providing confirmation and illustration where necessary or useful. Although motivation was the starting point for the research, the process was also successful in eliciting a broad range of information about the nature of pupils' learning experiences, their perceptions of aspects of modern language learning, and the factors giving rise to these — all essential pre-requisites for motivational analysis.

It was clear that the individual pupils were doing their best to give helpful and honest answers. But, as stated earlier, they may have been affected to some extent by the interview situation and by the enjoyable experience of being listened to at some length. It could be argued that as a result of all this the pupils might have given more positive answers to some questions, especially the later ones, than might have been expected. However, the strong messages about their learning experiences and the problems they meet remain clear and unaffected.

The research team has sought to give shape to all this, adding comments and suggesting some conclusions on the basis of the work done with these particular pupils. If these pupils are indeed representative of many, the team's observations might well be more generally applicable, though evidence for such a judgement would need to be established separately.

Section

4 ▶ The pupils' responses

The responses to each question are given in terms of statistics and trends, so that the main messages emerge as clearly as possible. Where numbers of pupils are given, these are followed by a percentage equivalent if the number is greater than ten, e.g. '27 pupils (44%) said they understood.'

Any further comments added are intended to promote further reflection and to identify possible issues for broader conclusions and/or investigation. Many of these are included or subsumed in Section 6 (Discussion of findings).

Question group A: preference

For Questions 1 and 2 only, the following abbreviations are used: MA (mathematics); EN (English); ML (modern language); FR (French); GE (German); SC (science); GG (geography); HI (history); TE (technology). For ML, pupils could only select the language they had been learning since Year 7. The seven subjects were selected as those in which possible issues of natural talent would be less likely to arise than in, for instance, music, art or physical education.

Question 1   **Put these subjects in order of preference (using cards): mathematics, English, French or German (as applied in individual cases), science, geography, history, technology.** *(Ask individually)*

Table 1: Number of top placings given			
Subject	**Boys***	**Girls***	**Total b + g***
EN	6	10	16
TE	10	5	15
SC	7	4	11
MA	3	6	9
HI	6	3	9
GG	2	4	6
ML (FR or GE)	0	5	5

* The total number of first placings in each column is greater than the number of pupils because some placed two or three subjects equal first.

Table 2: Frequency with which ML was given each of the popularity placings from 1 (top) to 7 (bottom)			
ML listed as	**Boys**	**Girls**	**Total**
1	0	5	5
2	4	1	5
3	5	3	8
4	8	8	16
5	7	7	14
6	4	4	8
7	3	3	6

Table 3: Frequency with which all subjects (including ML) were given each of the popularity placings, for comparative purposes (total numbers only):

Subject	Placed 1	Placed 2	Placed 3	Placed 4	Placed 5	Placed 6	Placed 7
EN	16	9	11	13	6	4	3
MA	9	8	7	11	6	16	5
SC	11	15	7	5	10	9	5
TE	15	10	6	8	3	6	14
HI	9	13	9	7	4	11	9
GG	6	4	7	8	12	11	14
ML	5	5	8	16	14	8	6

Table 4: Overall rank order for the 7 subjects

Subject	Points	Position
EN	302	1
SC	275	2
TE	262	3
HI	257	4
MA	245	5
ML	237	6
GG	205	7

The above was calculated on the basis of 7 points being awarded to a subject each time it was placed first, 6 points for each second placing, 5 points for each third placing, etc.

Comments on Question 1

Although Table 4 shows a relatively low overall rating for ML, the other tables highlight important factors which provide detail and shading in this picture. Table 1 shows a difference between boys and girls in that no boys placed ML as their first choice. This must affect overall rankings, on this sample at least. However, Table 2 shows a much more even spread between the genders, with an overall weighting towards the middle/lower rankings. Apart from the differences in places 1 and 2, there is remarkably little difference by gender: nine boys and nine girls rank ML 1, 2 or 3; places 4, 5, 6 and 7 are identical. Table 3 appears to support this, from a slightly different angle: the popularity profile for ML is more even and consistent than for some other subjects, lacking the extremes of technology and the heavy lower placings for geography.

Question 2 **Why do you prefer the subject you've put as no. 1?**
(Ask individually)

The figures in brackets indicate the number of times a particular reason was mentioned or could reasonably be identified or inferred. A range of reasons for preferences emerged. The popularity of English was based on an enjoyment of reading, drama, writing, stories and poems (24). Pupils referred to subjects being generally interesting, exciting, enjoyable (23). Science and technology placings relate to an interest in active work involving making, experimenting, and practical work (21). Variety of learning emerged as important across a range of subjects (20). For some pupils preferences were linked to a liking for the teacher (10) and being good at a subject (8). Only 3 pupils mentioned importance for a future career, although in response to other interview questions many pupils said they thought foreign languages important for career purposes. The fact that ML was a new subject at secondary school was important for three of the five pupils who placed ML first. As might be expected, overall preferences are clearly linked to pupils' actual experiences of a subject rather than their perception of its importance.

Question group B: modern language lessons

Question 3   **Do you think that you are doing well in (French/ German)? Why (not)?** *(Ask individually)*

This question was designed to shift the focus of the interview towards modern languages. 22 pupils (35%; 12 girls, 10 boys) said they thought they were doing well. 27 (44%; 14 girls, 13 boys) thought they were doing fairly or averagely well. 13 (21%; 5 girls, 8 boys) said they were not doing well. On this basis girls take, rightly or wrongly, a more positive view of their standard and progress than do boys.

Pupils mentioned a wide range of factors when explaining their view of their standard, though not all found it easy to give reasons. Responses referred not only to what it was pupils found hard or easy to do in modern languages but also to how they knew what their standard was, via teachers' comments, test results, or the set they were in. However, this varied according to how well pupils thought they were doing. Comparative data for other subjects was not to hand at the time of the project but would no doubt be illuminating.

11 pupils (18%) who claimed to be doing well or averagely well mentioned marks and test results, feedback from or positive regard for the teacher, and a sense of enjoyment. 9 pupils (15%) referred to the specific skills of speaking, reading and writing and said they felt they were quite good at these, or found them hard but could do them. None mentioned listening as a skill, this being apparently subsumed under understanding.

The 13 pupils who said they were not doing well gave a mixture of responses. Only 1 mentioned teacher feedback or marks, and comments often referred to what they found hard about modern language learning, though in a fairly general way: understanding generally what was going on; understanding words,

> *The first time I revised I came top of the class in a test. I'd been grounded so I stayed in and did some work. I achieved something.*

text and teacher; difficulty in producing language, especially at sentence level. Only 1 pupil mentioned recall and remembering as a problem. Some answered briefly, not very articulately, or in a rather negative tone. Others expressed a sense of dissatisfaction or

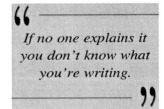

If no one explains it you don't know what you're writing.

even distrust: they felt they were not doing well even though they had been advised that they were through tests and via reports. 2 of the pupils with a community language were explicit about this.

Given the emphasis on pupil involvement with assessment and the nature of the National Curriculum level descriptions, it is interesting that pupils did not refer (in their own terms) to language becoming more complex, producing longer utterances, tackling longer reading or listening texts, working more independently, or building up a larger bank of language over time.

NB: Questions 4–8 inclusive are linked; they focus on what pupils do in modern language lessons, whether they enjoy them, and whether they find them helpful. The answers to these questions were entered as ticks on a grid, included in the Appendix. The basic list of 25 activities is also given below. Pupils' additional comments on Questions 7 and 8 were noted separately.

Question 4 **What kind of things do you do in your (French/ German) lessons?** *(Ask as a pair; tick from list)*

List of language learning activities:

- answering the teacher's questions
- repeating what you hear
- copying from the board or from a book
- listening to the teacher explain things
- working through the textbook
- listening to a tape
- listening to a native speaker of the foreign language in person
- drawing and labelling

- doing exercises, e.g. gap filling, true/false, matching things
- vocabulary tests
- reading short passages
- reading longer passages — more than a page
- working things out, e.g. how words sound, why some words have different endings
- being creative, e.g. making up a conversation, writing something of your own
- acting — role play
- reading aloud
- giving a spoken presentation to the class
- playing games
- singing
- using computers
- using dictionaries
- using video
- learning about the foreign country
- working with a partner
- working in groups

These 25 classroom activities are described in general terms which pupils were likely to recognise, rather than in terms of the National Curriculum programme of study or attainment targets. It includes examples of teaching activities, learning/practice activities, and tasks/assessment items. Pupils were asked to identify those things which happened fairly regularly or (as with some of the less routine items such as video, computers, singing) had happened at least three or four times in the current year. They were also asked to name any activities not listed but which commonly featured in lessons, though none did so.

Defining classroom events in modern languages is often complex unless precise individual tasks or activities are taking place, such as a tape/listening test, because different strands are often present at the same time. As an example, 'working through the textbook' may be combined with 'answering the teacher's questions' and 'copying from the board or book'. However, pupils' responses confirmed that these are indeed representative activities, and in any case it was not the intention to produce a time allocation analysis. The 25 activities were listed in deliberately random order, so that pupils would not be influenced by any pattern emerging as they responded. Incidentally, 'working with a partner' does not refer to role play or having a dialogue in the foreign language with a partner; it refers to working with a neighbour or partner on the same piece of work such as a textbook reading/writing task, preparing answers to questions, etc. There is probably some overlap between 'being creative — making up a conversation' and 'acting — role play'; the distinction used was that role play is generally based on a set of prompts of different kinds provided by the teacher.

Table 5 puts the 25 activities in rank order of frequency, based on the percentage of pupils identifying them as things they did. Obviously this table indicates the extent to which these activities figure in the experiences only of the 62 pupils interviewed. It quite possibly gives a representative picture of what happens, and to what extent, in modern language classrooms generally, though a wider evidence base would be needed for any such judgement.

Pupils may of course do other things, and within each activity listed there may be variants, but nonetheless their broad perception of what they spend their time doing is generally as above. A number of anomalies emerged, most obviously the fact that only 1 of the 25 items appears to be done by all 62 pupils. Common sense would suggest, for example, that all pupils work through a textbook, listen to teachers' explanations, and do exercises; yet fewer than 100% say they do. This might be explained by pupils' interpreting the question slightly differently: some might have answered in the sense that 'yes, these things happen in our classroom', while others might have meant 'these are not things that I personally do — the teacher may ask questions but I don't answer them!'

There are some boy/girl discrepancies (of 16% and over) which might be related to the above or might simply show that different pupils recall different things. Not all girls list textbook work (ranked 3rd in Table 5), though all boys do; more girls than boys say they listen to

	Table 5: Language learning activities in rank order of frequency	
	Language learning activities	**% of pupils doing them**
1	copying from the board or from a book	100%
2	working with a partner	94%
3	working through the textbook	92%
4	answering the teacher's questions	90%
5	listening to the teacher explain things	89%
6	using dictionaries	89%
7	doing exercises, e.g. gap filling, true/false, matching things	84%
8	repeating what you hear	82%
9	listening to a tape	82%
10	being creative, e.g. making up a conversation, writing something of your own	81%
11	drawing and labelling	77%
12	working things out, e.g. how words sound, why some words have different endings	76%
13	reading short passages	74%
14	vocabulary tests	71%
15	reading aloud	68%
16	working in groups	53%
17	learning about the foreign country	47%
18	playing games	35%
19	listening to a native speaker of the foreign language in person	32%
20	giving a spoken presentation to the class	27%
21	reading longer passages — more than a page	21%
22	acting — role play	19%
23	using video	15%
24	using computers	11%
25	singing	5%

tapes (ranked 9th); more boys than girls say they work things out (ranked 12th). There is a large discrepancy in the frequency with which boys and girls say they listen to a native speaker in person (15 girls, 5 boys). This might be because some groups are taught regularly by native speakers, and/or because some pupils did not think their regular teacher counted in this sense. A more worrying explanation might that be that some boys did not realise their teacher was a native speaker.

The nature of the modern language learning experience of most of the pupils interviewed, for most of the time, seems to be characterised by a fairly standard range of processes. These are listed as approximately the first half of the items in Table 5. The first nine items listed cover amongst them — reassuringly perhaps — all four language skills. There is a noticeable dip after no. 17, with well under half the pupils listing items 18 to 25. Video and IT have apparently made little impact. Individual comparisons are informative: 77% of pupils do drawing and labelling, while only 32% have the opportunity to listen to a live native speaker. The number of pupils who mention working things out (76%) is perhaps surprisingly high, since elsewhere there is less evidence of independent working. The relatively low placings for items 19, 20 and 21 in Table 5 suggest that few of these pupils have had opportunities to work with longer texts or pieces in the foreign language.

NB: Questions 5–8 explore the extent to which pupils like or dislike the 25 activities and the extent to which they find them helpful or not. The responses are given as percentages of the number of pupils who said, in answer to Question 4, that these are things they do.

> Copying, not learning. Don't know what it means or how to pronounce it.

For example, 56 pupils out of the 62 pupils said in answer to Question 4 that they answer teachers' questions: this converts to 90%, as given in Table 5. In Question 5, 13 pupils said they liked doing this, giving a response of 13 out of 56 (not out of 62), which converts to 23%.

Table 6 sets out these and other correlations. It forms the statistical basis for the following comments on pupils' responses to Questions 5–8.

Table 6: Language learning activities

	Do	Like	Dislike
Answering the teacher's questions	56	13	7
Repeating what you hear	51	15	4
Copying from the board or from a book	62	11	17
Listening to the teacher explain things	55	8	1
Working through the textbook	57	15	9
Listening to a tape	51	23	4
Listening to a native speaker of the foreign language in person	20	6	0
Drawing and labelling	48	17	4
Doing exercises, e.g. gap filling, true/false, matching things	52	17	0
Vocabulary tests	44	11	10
Reading short passages	46	7	4
Reading longer passages — more than a page	13	3	1
Working things out, e.g. how words sound, why some words have different endings	47	8	2
Being creative, e.g. making up a conversation, writing something of your own	50	12	5
Acting — role play	12	8	3
Reading aloud	42	9	14
Giving a spoken presentation to the class	17	1	7
Playing games	22	9	0
Singing	3	0	2
Using computers	7	6	0
Using dictionaries	55	13	3
Using video	9	4	1
Learning about the foreign country	29	6	0
Working with a partner	58	25	3
Working in groups	33	14	3

Table 6: Language learning activities (continued)

	Help	Not help
Answering the teacher's questions	12	0
Repeating what you hear	23	1
Copying from the board or from a book	6	13
Listening to the teacher explain things	15	1
Working through the textbook	9	3
Listening to a tape	15	2
Listening to a native speaker of the foreign language in person	4	2
Drawing and labelling	4	7
Doing exercises, e.g. gap filling, true/false, matching things	5	2
Vocabulary tests	16	0
Reading short passages	8	1
Reading longer passages — more than a page	3	0
Working things out, e.g. how words sound, why some words have different endings	4	0
Being creative, e.g. making up a conversation, writing something of your own	2	0
Acting — role play	3	0
Reading aloud	6	0
Giving a spoken presentation to the class	2	0
Playing games	5	2
Singing	0	2
Using computers	0	2
Using dictionaries	11	2
Using video	3	1
Learning about the foreign country	2	1
Working with a partner	14	0
Working in groups	5	4

Question 5   **Which activities do you particularly like doing?**
                (Ask individually)

An overall picture of likes and dislikes is difficult to discern because of the varying numbers of pupils doing different activities: the fewer the pupils, the less secure the judgement. It would appear that pupils have no strong sense of either liking or disliking the great majority of things they do in the modern languages classroom. However, within those activities done by a significant number of pupils (at least half), three were particularly liked by over 40% of pupils doing them. These were: working with a partner, listening to a tape, and working in groups. No single common activity was explicitly identified as popular by more than 45% of pupils doing them. Very few pupils listed acting out, video and computers as regular activities, but most who did so enjoyed them.

> **"** *I enjoyed writing letters to send to people — not letters to really send but exciting because I knew I could send one.* **"**

Only two activities showed any noticeable difference between preferences of boys and girls. 8 boys liked reading aloud, while only 1 girl did so. 5 girls but only 1 boy liked learning about the foreign country. Otherwise the numbers for boys and girls were within 3 or 4.

Question 6   **Which activities do you dislike doing?** *(Ask individually)*

Few items were mentioned as being particularly disliked. 16 of the 25 activities were disliked by 10% or fewer of the pupils doing them. Of the most common activities (done by 50% of pupils or more), those most disliked were reading aloud (33% of 42 pupils), copying from board or book (27% of 62 pupils), and vocabulary tests (23% of 44 pupils). Among those activities less frequently done, spoken presentations were unpopular with 41% of 17 pupils, and acting out/role play was disliked by 25% of the 12 pupils (though actively enjoyed by almost all the others). Singing was strongly disliked by the few pupils involved.

27

Question 7   **Which of these activities help you to learn better?**
....   **How?** *(Ask individually)*

In their answers to Questions 7 and 8, pupils inevitably use words such as 'learn', 'understand' and 'know'. The interviewers deliberately did not define these words, whether used by them or by pupils, and pupils' use of them was accepted at its face value. It emerged that pupils use them with different meanings, as perhaps teachers and others do. As examples, 'learn' was perceived as meaning both 'memorise' and 'make progress'; 'understand' was used variously to refer to understanding (a) the foreign language or text, (b) what was going on in the lesson generally, (c) the teacher's instructions, or (d) how a point of language works.

As with likes and dislikes, pupils seemed more ready to identify things as helpful than unhelpful. This indicates an insecurity or immaturity of judgement, perhaps, but it also suggests that pupils are prepared to give teachers and the teaching the benefit of the doubt and to accept that something may be helpful even though they cannot at present see how. Common items readily seen as helpful include working with partners (24% of those doing it), listening to teachers' explanations (27%), repeating what is heard (45%), listening to tapes (29%), and vocabulary tests (36%). These also, importantly, score low on unhelpfulness, whereas pupils are more ambivalent towards, for example, working in groups and listening to native speakers.

> *Reading passages? In France you'd be speaking to people.*

In explaining why they found things helpful, pupils frequently answered fairly generally ('helps me learn', 'you understand it better'). But most distinguished, encouragingly, between activities such as vocabulary tests and exercises, which helped them see how well they were doing, and activities designed to help them progress. In addition, there were some perceptive comments about individual activities which showed a clear grasp of their value: repeating is linked to improved pronunciation, textbooks give useful examples of written language, answering teachers' questions promotes independence, reading helps with, for example, seeing how word order changes.

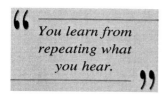

You learn from repeating what you hear.

Boys and girls broadly agreed in their views of whether and how activities were helpful, except for working with a partner, which was judged to be helpful by noticeably more boys than girls.

Question 8

Which of these activities do not help you to learn better? Explain. *(Ask individually)*

Few of the activities were considered by many pupils to be unhelpful. This is not always good news: 77% of pupils regularly draw and label, but only 15% of them found it an unhelpful practice. It could be argued that averagely attaining Year 9 pupils should not be doing this in lesson time. Conversely some claim that the pictures help with recall of vocabulary. 21% of pupils found copying from board or book unhelpful, mainly on the grounds that it is done as an unthinking process with no personal involvement and does not promote retention or understanding. Using computers was found unhelpful by 29% of pupils doing so (and positively helpful by none). Games were generally popular and judged quite helpful, but singing was dismissed out of hand, although again the numbers involved were small.

A wide range of reasons were given for why activities were unhelpful: drawing and labelling is not relevant to being in France; true/false exercises are not helpful when pupils do not find out why they made mistakes; some group work is affected by poor behaviour; textbooks do not explain things well; using a computer is not linked closely to language learning, or the task is minimal — 'copying what we wrote'; singing has no point.

A number of common activities did not attract any strong judgements as to their value, receiving low scores (10% or less) for both helpfulness and unhelpfulness. These include in particular doing exercises (scoring 10% and 4%); being creative and making up own conversation or writing (4% and 0%); and working things out (9% and 0%). Learning about the foreign country (7% and 3%), although less frequently done, was also in this category. There were no noticeable differences between boys and girls in terms of their responses to this question.

As an overall comment on responses to Questions 5–8, it is important to note that pupils readily distinguish between whether they like/dislike an activity and whether they find it helpful or not. They do not make a simplistic connection: vocabulary tests, for example, attract a fairly high unpopularity score but also score quite well on helpfulness.

Clearly things which score highly for enjoyment and helpfulness offer fertile ground for teachers, as long as teachers also see them as productive and use them appropriately. These include: working with a partner, repeating what is heard, and listening to tapes. Although video is used by few, it too scores highly in both respects. Acting/role play does well and is perhaps, interestingly, under-exploited. At the other extreme, copying from book or board is done frequently and does not score well for enjoyment or helpfulness. Some of the pupils using computers enjoy doing so but do not find the experience helpful.

Question 9 **Think back to your last lesson. Were you clear what you were supposed to learn from it? (Ask individually. Push towards 'learn', rather than 'do'.)**

This question was carefully worded and the interviewers steered pupils towards the focus of learning rather than the basic content or activities of the lesson. Nonetheless — or perhaps because of this — it did not prove an easy one for many pupils to answer: only 2 pupils said 'yes' explicitly, and even then their comments were imprecise. Pupils tended to describe what they learnt (or did), rather than stating whether they were clear on they were supposed to have learnt. (In some schools the most recent lessons had been given over to tests or revision, or had been cover lessons. This may have affected the recollections of the 20 pupils (32%) involved.)

There were 20 references to what the lesson was about, in terms of topic areas such as clothes and colours. 7 pupils spoke in terms of 'learning how to say or talk about . . . ' In 6 cases pupils mentioned points of grammar, but with little precision or apparent understanding: they referred to 'nouns, adjectives and stuff'. 2 mentioned a mnemonic for '*être*' verbs in French — 'the Mr Vandertramps thing' — but in a very confused manner. 1 pupil mentioned using a dictionary and pronunciation. 5 talked about learning new words but only 3 could recall any of these. 20 (32%) mentioned work on skills (reading, writing). 2 pupils mentioned learning in a different sense: finding out that s/he was good at numbers, or realising that one must not waste time.

15 pupils (24%) said that in the last lesson they had learnt nothing or very little that was new, sometimes because work had been done earlier and/or was already known. In 49 cases pupils did not talk about what learning had been intended, or achieved by them. Instead they simply described or mentioned things they did in the lesson, often in very sketchy terms.

Overall, the pupils were not well equipped to talk about learning objectives, even in simple terms, in a way appropriate to their age and stage. Most simply said what the lesson was about, in terms of topics or routine activities. Their attempts to talk about the work were affected either by unclear recall or understanding of the work or by an inability to articulate or describe its purpose, or both. There was little sense that pupils understood that lessons contain a number of working levels or areas ('through clothes we learnt about how to state preferences, use some new verbs, use adjectives,' etc). Indeed there was little overall sense of pupils understanding in simple but coherent terms what learning a language actually means. Many referred to activities of various types but gave little idea of what was to be learnt by doing them. Pupils seem rarely to have access to 'advance organisers' of any type, for example in the form of a guide to lesson content and activity sequence written on the blackboard by teachers.

It might be unrealistic or unnecessary to expect more, and the same issue might well apply to other subjects. Either way it is disturbing that many of the pupils interviewed had little by way of a clear view of what they were supposed to have learnt from a typical lesson, even in terms, for example, of new words acquired.

Question 10

If answer to 9 is 'Yes': Did you succeed? How do you know? If answer is 'No': What did you learn? *(Ask individually. Push towards 'learn', rather than 'do'.)*

Most pupils offered a straight answer to this question, despite (or perhaps because of) their vagueness in responding to the previous one. 33 pupils (53%) said they felt they had succeeded in learning what was being taught; 4 said they had not; 19 (31%) said they had to some extent; 7 gave no response or did not know.

The supplementary questions, however, revealed that some of this confidence was misplaced. Very few pupils could give any direct evidence that they had retained items of language which they could now recall. Their judgements as to whether they had succeeded in learning were based on factors such as: ability to complete the task or activity; mark achieved for test or homework; teacher's response; finding the work easy; getting most of the questions right. Some pupils felt they had succeeded because they had coped with the lesson generally and understood what was going on. Those who had done tests quoted the marks and standard they achieved as evidence of having succeeded in learning.

Failure to succeed in learning was interpreted as, or associated with, failure to complete tasks, or having to ask for help. Many pupils observed of their own accord that they could remember little by way of new language from what they had done. Some who had spent the previous lesson carrying out tasks such as designing a poster or even producing a revision booklet could not say whether they had learnt anything or not.

On the whole pupils were reasonably confident that they were making progress, but this is largely on the basis of their performance in the lesson rather than because they had clearly mastered and remembered items of language which they could recall and apply when required in future.

Question 11   **What is the best thing you have achieved in your (Fr/Ge) work so far?** *(Ask individually)*

Positive responses were given by 49 pupils (79%); 13 pupils (21%) could not recall anything they had achieved of particular merit. The positive answers could be categorised under a number of overall headings: performing to others (plays, interviews, tapes), and display work; heavy emphasis on productive skills (speaking, or writing a letter that could be sent abroad); high marks or test results; being in a top set earlier on; doing something very different from usual. Almost all pupils referred back to events or achievements in Years 7 and 8 rather than the current year. Singing was mentioned by some pupils, despite their dismissal of it in Questions 5–8.

Many pupils interpreted the question as referring to pupils' favourite or most enjoyable experience in modern languages, rather than the highest standard of work they had produced. Thus they mentioned activities or events in class (shopping scenes, acting out, French breakfasts) rather than achievements or successes on the part of the individual pupil. Others referred to achievement indirectly, in terms of doing a test well or being in a higher set.

15 pupils (24%) mentioned a point of linguistic achievement in modern languages of which they were proud and which they had enjoyed. These included: making up a poem involving verb endings, making a spoken presentation to the class, performing a conversation made up by them, writing a practice letter well, standard of speaking improving, doing well in a French quiz, feeling able to cope in France, increased spoken fluency, writing independently a long letter to a pen-friend, learning to write longer passages, making an extended tape about themselves. One pupil had been enabled, through the presence and help of a French partner in the classroom, to understand for the first time how French definite articles work, an example of genuinely intrinsic motivation born of direct contact with a native speaker. These examples highlighted the motivational influence of real achievement of a worthwhile task, completion of which had clearly boosted the self-esteem of the pupils concerned.

Question group C: language learning

Question 12   **What do you need in order to learn a language well?** *Suggested prompt:* **For instance, you may need to have a good memory. What other skills might you need?**

This question sought to explore not only pupils' views of what attributes and skills are needed, but also to some extent whether pupils think they can acquire them. If they feel they cannot, then this might indicate that they see language learning, to some extent at least, as something which is inherently beyond them; they will have developed the view that (a) there is such a thing as linguistic aptitude, (b) it is an absolute, and (c) it is possessed by others but not by them. This will clearly affect motivation.

56 of the 62 pupils (90%) were able to suggest at least one factor associated with successful language learning, and 49 pupils (79%) offered more than one. Six pupils could not think of anything. To a large extent pupils were offering descriptions of good language learners and/or were identifying the aspects of language learning in which they felt deficient, rather than identifying desirable personal attributes. As an example, many pupils find pronunciation difficult (see Question 13) and say this is an essential skill. However, they were clearly answering on the basis of their honest observation and reflection.

> " *Writing your own passages, and making own conversations means you're working things out. Thinking things through for yourself. Helps you understand it more as you go along.* "

The following factors were mentioned most frequently (sometimes in different words), with the number of times they were mentioned given in brackets: concentration (12); patience/self-discipline/willingness to practise (11); a good ear/listening skills (11); ability to pronounce (linked to reading the written word aloud) (9); positive attitude/motivation, willingness to work (8); ability to use the language, manipulate it, independently (7); ability to plan, review, revise work, and ask for/get help (6). Other suggestions made by 1 or 2 pupils included: ability to write accurately; ability to express oneself when speaking; dictionary skills. Pupils did not mention memory because this was the example given by the interviewer.

Some of the more general factors mentioned apply to any subject, but 26 pupils (42%) referred specifically to one or other linguistic area such as grammar, pronunciation, accents (written), careful listening, and (in their own terms) verb conjugations and endings.

The factors mentioned can be grouped under four main headings: linguistic aptitude (defined as an individual's particular facility for language learning which enables a relatively high rate of progress to be made), language-specific skills, general study and organisational skills, and attitude and other affective factors. There were no significant gender differences.

Pupils did not in practice distinguish between the skills of using a language and those of **learning** a language. Again, perhaps this is more than can be expected at this stage. As an example, pronunciation is considered to be something at which one is either good or not; pupils do not seem to think in terms of **learning** how to pronounce well, as an accessible process. This suggests that pupils do indeed regard some aspects of language learning as dependent on the possession or otherwise of a specific aptitude or facility.

Question 13 **What sort of problems do you come across when you are trying to learn?** *(Ask as a pair)*

The question refers to 'problems' without specifying further what was meant. In this open context, pupils often talked about things they find difficult in modern language learning, rather than barriers or obstacles, but nonetheless everything mentioned was clearly a factor which affected progress.

27 different factors were mentioned, some general, some very specific and detailed, the latter sometimes offered as examples of the kind of

> **I find it hard, but the teacher doesn't think that I do.**

thing which affects learning. Clearly many items mentioned are linked or can be categorised under the same heading. However, two items occurred frequently: pronunciation was mentioned by 21 pupils (34%), and failure to understand words or phrases (whether spoken or written) by 10. Pupils talked about writing in various ways: writing generally (4); spelling (7); umlauts and accents on letters (7). Long words were a problem for 5 pupils. Points of grammar emerged as regular and irregular verbs (5); gender (4); rules generally (2); making sentences (4). Only 1 pupil said any particular topic (directions) was more difficult than any other.

Class disruption was mentioned by 8 pupils, and memory problems by 6. Other general problems, mentioned at most by 2 pupils, were: lack of confidence, insufficient time, changes of teacher, lack of reading, lessons badly organised. Self-evidently the fact that only a few pupils mentioned problems with grammar, for example, does not mean that no other pupils have such problems.

Significantly, many pupils appear to be failing to get past what to them are crucial obstacles of sounds, meanings and spellings. They feel they lack the confidence or skills to acquire language from exposure to its everyday use in the classroom or from the textbook in any kind of large-scale, extended or gist context: they tend to find problems at the level of the single word or even syllable. They identify problems in sharp and clear terms of these fundamental aspects of language, rather than for instance topics or even activities and tasks they commonly do: they are in their own way very clear on what they feel they lack. To this extent the 'chunk' approach as they experience it does not enable them to progress in terms of manipulating or extending or recombining the chunks to build independently more complex items of language, on the basis of clearly understood linguistic principles.

There is little correspondence between their answers here and those relating to Questions 9 and 10, about what they were supposed to learn in their last lesson: there, most claimed to have succeeded, though here they identified numerous basic areas on which they feel they need help. One pupil (a community language user) articulated her frustration at some length:

'Usually when I can't do something I can't really explain to the teacher where I get stuck and what I can't do. That's what I need, more confidence to go up to the teacher and say: 'I don't understand this bit'; because I just say: 'I don't understand this question', and she just explains what the question is. But then it really is that I can't answer the question. I understand the question. I can't write it down in French . . . I can't write — I can't answer it.'

Question 14   **When you have a problem, do you usually get enough help of the sort you need?** *(Ask as a pair)*

Interestingly, in the light of their answers to Question 13, 49 pupils (79%) said fairly directly that they received enough help. 5 said they did not, and a further 5 hedged somewhat but were really saying no. Three pupils said they sometimes got enough help. One pupil referred to people not wishing to look stupid by asking for help.

There seems to be some discrepancy between the problems and the help given, in that the problems clearly do not go away. It may be that the pupils receive much help from teachers, but of the kind needed to help them past the immediate barrier rather than help them to cope with the same or related difficulties in future.

Question 15   **Where do you get help?** *(Ask as a pair)*

Most pupils mentioned a number of sources of help. Self-evidently perhaps the teacher was the prime source, mentioned by 48 pupils (77%) — the same group largely who answered yes to the previous question. These pupils often mentioned asking for help with pronunciation. 14 pupils (23%), surprisingly perhaps, did not refer to the teacher as a prime source of help.

37

31 (50%) mentioned friends or partners in class; 23 (37%) referred to dictionaries and 20 (32%) to textbooks, usually the glossary, to look up words. 10 pupils mentioned family and relatives. 11 pupils (18%) explicitly referred to self-help: checking and working things out for themselves (6); using the class display (2); listening to others' responses (1); using a help-sheet (1). One pupil mentioned going to the library for books and tapes. Otherwise independent working does not figure largely.

There is a clear link with Questions 13 and 14 in that pupils most often mentioned getting or looking for help with pronunciation, meanings and spellings, in other words at a primary level of contact with the language. At least if they are looking for help with these areas it suggests most pupils think they can raise their standard. However, the nature of the help sought seems frequently to relate to getting the current task completed rather than securing understanding on a longer term basis. There was no reference to help with dealing with longer pieces of language or texts, or skills development, or producing more complex language, or in a general sense finding out what a quality response or piece of work would be.

> *Listening to the teacher explain things means 'you get attached to what the work is all about'.*

Incidental questions

Q*uestion 16*

How do you organise your work — books, folders, etc.? *Ask if necessary:*
- **do you have places for recording vocabulary, grammar?** *(Ask as a pair)*
- **could you find all your old exercise books/ folders if asked?** *(Ask individually)*
- **do you ever use your old exercise books/ folders? If so, how?** *(Ask individually)*

The three supplementary questions above were used with all pupils. The information in this area was difficult to extract and analyse largely because of the lack of consistency in the way in which pupils build up, organise and use their body of written material (notes, vocabulary lists, etc.) over time. In some cases it appeared that organisational formats varied within individual schools. Pupils were not asked to bring their notebooks with them.

For recording vocabulary and grammar notes, the normal pattern is for pupils to work through their exercise books, noting things as they go, though there were many small exceptions or variations to this pattern. The reference to grammar was explicitly understood by few pupils: the great majority talked in terms of topic notes, words, English work, French work, rough work, neat work.

21 pupils (34%) said there was a place at the back of their exercise books for vocabulary, though it did not emerge how they actually noted this. 11 pupils (18%) said they had separate vocabulary books, some saying they could provide these for themselves if they wished (practice here varied within schools). 8 pupils referred to a further range of items variously entered at the back: rough work, homework, tests, English. 7 pupils also mentioned loose sheets and folders containing topic tests and other items, but again the picture varied within schools. 2 pupils mentioned other items: tapes from the library or shop-bought, and computer disks.

41 pupils (66%) said they could find all their old exercise books, and 11 (18%) said they could find some. 10 pupils said they did not still have them, or were not sure. 2 pupils said their teacher had them. Those pupils who still had their exercise books said they used them in homework revising a topic or to look up words when preparing a conversation (18 — 29%); in revision for tests (14 — 23%); or out of curiosity, to see how they had progressed (7). None referred to using them to help with points of structure or grammar.

Pupils said much about copying from textbook and board in their answers to Questions 4–8. The end use of much of that copying is difficult to see on the basis of their answers to Question 16. It would be necessary to observe pupils at work directly in order to see exactly how they make and use their notes and other materials, but it is difficult to discern a systematic pattern of guidance and practice here.

Do you use a textbook in lessons? Is it helpful? How? *(Ask as a pair)*

All pupils said they use a textbook in lessons regularly or sometimes. A few pupils mentioned how books were used in lessons to accompany work such as listening to tapes, but almost all answered the follow-up questions as required in terms of how helpful they personally found them as support for modern language learning.

Most gave a number of examples of how books help them to learn. In total 23 identifiably different reasons were given, though some of these related more to how they were used in class (with tapes, or as the basis for teacher explanation).

By far the most commonly quoted use of a textbook was as a source of help with vocabulary: 29 pupils (47%) referred to words at the back, word lists, glossaries, index, dictionary sections. 12 pupils (19%) referred to end-of-unit revision sections, 'Flash grammaire', 'Station service', and similar. 7 pupils said that textbooks were 'generally' helpful. Other examples given, with numbers of pupils quoting them in brackets, were: helpful with spelling (4); helpful when doing exercises (4); pictures and sentences help understanding (4); helpful for reading foreign handwriting (3). Other factors were quoted only by 1 or 2 pupils: writing labels; boxes with key words; grammar and sentence-building; gives phrases to learn; teaches about the foreign country.

9 pupils said the books were not helpful or were otherwise deficient in some respects: 2 mentioned the stories in them as boring, 2 said the books did not explain things.

Pupils see many different uses for their textbook. They clearly turn to them primarily as sources of information about words, their meaning, and to a lesser extent their use. This would correspond to their responses to Question 13 about the problems they meet. Logically, books are seen as helpful for aspects of writing. Clearly few pupils use books for browsing or as an aid to independent working beyond what is required for homework. Only 1 pupil referred to the textbook helping with grammar and sentence-building: this is in line with the few references in Question 13 to these areas being problems for pupils. Pupils did not indicate that they considered their textbooks to be interesting, stimulating, or enjoyable.

Question 18 **Do you have your own textbook?** *(Ask as a pair)*

36 pupils (58%) answered yes; 22 (35%) answered no. 4 pupils said they were issued with textbooks if homework required their use. In the case of 2 schools some pupils had their own textbooks while others did not. Clearly the range of homework pupils can be offered, and any memorising work based on an accurate model, will be affected by this. All pupils could name the book they used. A very wide range of textbooks is in use as standard mainstream provision.

Question group D: progress

Question 19 **You have been learning (Fr/Ge) for nearly three years now. Do you think that the standard of your work is getting higher?** *If answer is 'Yes':* **In what way?** *Possible prompt:* **For instance, you may be expected to speak for longer or to write more words on a topic about yourself.** *(Ask as a pair)*

As a general response, 49 (79%) pupils said they had progressed and their standard had risen. 11 (17%) felt they had made only a little progress, or qualified their description of their improved standard in some way. Only 1 pupil said he had not really improved. 2 said they had progressed, but their further comments did not tally with this.

Pupils expressed the nature of their progress variously. 2 said how well they thought they were doing in each of the four skills, but the majority spoke in terms of speaking and writing only, using the word 'more' as a key indicator: they can use more and longer words. 4 said explicitly this is how they know their standard is higher. 10 pupils referred to having longer conversations, and 12 (19%) to being able to pronounce better. 2 pupils mentioned improved confidence in speaking. Writing was associated for 6 pupils with producing longer sentences; 5 referred also to sentences being more complex. 1 spoke of putting phrases together, another about forming sentences 'but not in the way Sir does'.

Through these and similar comments it is clear that some pupils are developing a sense of language coming together in longer chunks, though few are aware of the issue of increasing complexity. Only 3 pupils mentioned aspects of grammar: 2 mentioned verbs getting harder, and 1 spoke of problems with 'little words' such as 'à la'. Some pupils mentioned understanding better but it was not clear whether this referred to understanding the spoken/written foreign language, or how the foreign language worked, or simply what was going on. Only 2 mentioned understanding a French person, and only 2 mentioned reading.

Pupils also mentioned other indicators which to them showed their standard was rising but which were not as closely language-related. 5 pupils said they were now getting better marks, and 3 had moved to a higher set. 3 said the work was getting harder, and 2 said they knew more about France. 5 mentioned improved written presentation.

Pupils found this question hard to answer in any way which did not relate to, for example, marks attained or test results. Perhaps this difficulty reflects a general uncertainty among pupils as to what constitutes learning and, especially, progress in a foreign language. Despite the recent emphasis on assessment, it was not evident that pupils had a clear and accurate view of how they were doing.

Question 20   **How does your teacher help you to raise the standard of your work?** *(Ask as a pair — refer back to points made on previous question)*

Pupils gave a wide range of examples of what teachers do to help them improve. 31 pupils (50%) talked about teachers setting higher expectations: making the work harder, telling pupils to write more than the minimum required, linking in earlier work, correcting, promoting independent thinking/working, showing how to produce better language. 22 (35%) mentioned direct explicit explanations and support, individual attention, help after absence, and clear introductions and explanations of the work and tasks. It must be a cause for concern that teachers were also described as helping with target language issues by translating into English their own instructions which they have just given in the foreign language.

15 (23%) referred to motivational factors: being encouraging, promoting fun and enjoyment, giving merit marks. 8 pupils mentioned regular tests. 7 spoke of teachers generally promoting high standards through insistence on good presentation, accuracy, homework completed, requiring work to be redone. Only 3 pupils said their teacher did not really help them to improve.

Despite the range of answers, pupils needed much prompting for this question, which is a fundamental one about the teaching they receive. On the whole they accept that their teachers want them to improve their standard, but there is no reference, for example, to teachers giving pupils specific learning skills or techniques. It may be that, as in their answers to Questions 13 and 14, pupils are describing in some of their answers here the kind of short-term help they need with specific problems. There is a difference between helping to do work and helping them to become better at doing it on their own. However, the references to rising expectations and to the more complex work presented are positive.

Question group E: attitudes

Question 21   **Do you think it is important to learn a foreign language?** *(Ask individually)*

This is a question about one aspect of extrinsic motivation. Pupils were not asked for reasons for their answers, but all offered at least one reason for their view whatever their response. 45 pupils (72%) said definitely yes. 8 pupils (13%) said basically no. 9 pupils (15%) gave a qualified yes: i.e. languages are important generally but not for them personally, or are important only if one is going to go or work abroad regularly.

By far the most commonly quoted reason for the importance of learning a foreign language was that of jobs/employment, both generally (30 pupils — 48%) or specifically if working abroad (6). 9 pupils mentioned visits or holidays abroad, and 9 said, in their own terms, that it enables one to have direct contact with other peoples. 5 pupils said languages are an important qualification to have. 5 pupils said languages are important because one does not know what will be needed for the future, and they might go abroad. 4 pupils mentioned a family or other personal connection of different kinds: some had relatives with language-related skills or jobs, others mentioned helping a relative when abroad or with a foreign contact. Other factors mentioned by individual pupils were the EU, the ability to read newspapers, and the value of modern languages learning as mind training.

During their answers to this question a number of pupils made other comments of a general nature about the value of language learning. These included: the need to know more than one foreign language (3); the importance of languages for specific jobs such as translators, travel agents (3); everyone should know at least one other language (1); some languages are more important than others (3); and a comment that the rest of the world speaks English, French, German or Spanish, so one needs English plus one of these.

The message that pupils have received most clearly about the importance of learning a language is rather utilitarian in tone. References to the social and cultural advantages of learning a language are fewer than might have been expected or wished. The issue of importance for jobs is unlikely to be sustained for all pupils, and is unlikely to continue to motivate them throughout their secondary schooling. However, in overall terms the response to this question was strongly positive and indicates the extent to which pupils accept the place of languages on the curriculum. Schools and teachers have

> *I remember a French quiz in the school magazine. Out of the lower school I was the only person in Year 9 to win a prize.*

clearly succeeded in communicating to pupils a sense of the importance of languages as a life skill. This source of extrinsic motivation is a powerful one. Given the background of the pupils, it was encouraging that many have in this respect quite a wide world view. Only 1 pupil said languages were a waste of time; even those who said these external factors did not presently apply to them said that languages were important for those involved in work abroad or similar, and that languages might be important later in their lives. 8 pupils offered a strongly personal statement or anecdote, and no pupils seemed indifferent to the issue: every pupil had an opinion.

Question 22 **What do your parents think about your learning a foreign language?** *(Ask individually)*

The parents themselves were not consulted. These responses reflect only therefore pupils' knowledge or opinion of what their parents think. This would again count as an important extrinsic motivator for many pupils.

There was some overlap among the different responses to this question. 21 pupils (32%) could not give an answer because this was not a matter they had discussed at home. It would be inappropriate to make assumptions about this in terms of whether it might denote parental indifference or not, but it is perhaps worth bearing in mind that the pupils were being interviewed at a crucial stage in their education.

By the majority of pupils (61%), parental attitudes were described in various terms as positive (48%) or very positive (13%). Only 3 pupils said their parents were explicitly indifferent towards their learning a language, though a further 3 said their parents had a view about the importance of different languages. 4 pupils said their parents had mentioned the importance of languages for jobs. No parent was reported as saying explicitly that foreign language learning was a waste of time.

15 pupils (24%) referred to the family as providing a context for their language use/learning. Some parents/relatives had learned a language

or used one in their job or social life and encouraged or helped the pupils concerned. Some pupils were proud of being able to teach their parents or help them while abroad. 3 pupils had a mixed-nationality (e.g. Franco-Italian) relative. 1 pupil had modern languages computer disks at home, though these were not further specified. Another referred illuminatingly to the fact that his family was Tunisian and spoke French at home, so they never spoke about modern languages learning!

Taken together, the responses to this question and to Question 21 reflect a strongly positive set of attitudes towards the importance of language learning among learners and their families.

Question 23 **Do you think (girls) are better at language learning than (boys)?** *(Ask question both ways round)* **Explain.** *(Ask as a pair)*

This question was asked largely to gauge the pupils' response to the issue as a whole, to see if it seemed important to them. Some showed by the way they answered that they thought the question was irrelevant and, beyond that, inappropriate and politically incorrect. However, the question also highlights pupils' perceptions, in their own terms, of the twin issues of attitude and aptitude, in particular the commonly held view that aptitude is a fixed and somehow pre-determined quality, an absolute which one either owns or lacks and which cannot be acquired or improved. In this respect the pupils were refreshingly unaffected by common stereotypes.

44 pupils (71% — 20 girls and 24 boys) said there were no differences. 17 pupils (27% — 10 girls and 7 boys) said they thought girls were better. 1 girl was unsure, but based her response on the number of boys in top sets rather than other factors. No pupil thought boys were better than girls. 1 or 2 girls commented that boys could do better if they tried or were interested.

Pupils who said girls were better expressed their reasons both in terms of how girls were better and how boys were worse. The number of pupils giving each reason is in brackets.

In terms of **girls being better,** reasons given by **girls** were that girls listen (2); concentrate better (2); settle down to work (2); learn better (1); have a better memory (1). Reasons given by **boys** were that girls are better at listening (2); concentrate more (1); have a better attitude (1); pick things up quicker (1); are friends with the teacher (1); 'are better at that sort of thing' (1); and that there are more girls in the top set.

In terms of **boys being worse,** reasons given by **girls** were that boys 'muck around' (5); are not interested (2); prefer drama and acting (1); and argue about who is going to read out (1). Reasons given by **boys** were that boys 'muck around' (5); think they know it all and don't need to listen (1); think they are better although they are not (1).

It would be unreasonable to expect more by way of explanation for pupils' views than that given here, based, as it is, on overall impressions and day-to-day classroom experience. The key factors, in the opinion of almost all these latter pupils and by some who think there is no difference in standard, relate to matters of attitude and behaviour. Only 1 pupil — a boy — mentioned girls as being in some unspecified way better at language learning in itself: the natural aptitude argument. Girls emerge as seeming to be more compliant and disciplined. No pupil said or appeared to imply that languages were in any way 'a girls' subject'; this is perhaps supported by the gender picture in Question 1, where apart from the absence of top placings by boys the popularity of languages was broadly the same among boys and girls. On closer analysis, pupils of both sexes appear to be saying that if girls are better at learning a language than boys it is because they spend more of the available time actively engaged in doing so.

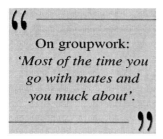

On groupwork:
'Most of the time you go with mates and you muck about'.

Question 24 How did you feel about your first ever foreign language lesson? *(Ask individually)*

Individual pupils talked in terms both of their feelings before their first modern languages lesson and their response to it when it actually happened, depending on what they could remember and what their

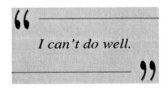

I can't do well.

overriding impression was. Only 4 pupils could not recall their response to their first foreign language lesson. The most common reaction, mentioned by 27 pupils (44%), was one of apprehension and nervousness (often due to direct contact with teachers using the target language). In almost all cases pupils said they were quickly reassured, albeit sometimes by teachers using English. 14 pupils (23%) said they had felt excited and looked forward to it. 8 remembered a sense of fun and enjoyment. 7 other pupils described a positive reaction (interesting, difficult but good, easy, proud to be doing it).

7 pupils said explicitly that they had responded negatively (were not interested, did not want to do it, waste of time, felt depressed, found it hard). 1 pupil reported no special feelings either way.

The remarkable thing here was that so many pupils claimed to remember a lesson or lessons from almost three years previously and their feelings about the experience. If the group who say their initial apprehension was allayed is counted as giving a response in the positive/neutral range, this leaves only 7 pupils (11%) with an abiding negative memory.

Question 25 Have your feelings changed? If yes: (a) in what way? (b) why? *(Ask individually)*

On the basis of their responses to the previous question, 22 pupils (35%) said that their feelings towards modern languages learning were now more positive; 17 (27%) said their feelings were now less positive; and 23 (37%) said their feelings were much the same as they had been. The overall boy/girl balance in each category is broadly equal.

The 35% of pupils who were now feeling more positive gave a fairly consistent set of reasons: feeling more capable and confident (7); seeing the use of modern languages more (6); making progress in what they know and understand (5); the work becoming easier (3). Also mentioned by 1 or 2 pupils were the work getting harder (as a plus point); feeling able to go to France and chat; working together or in more detail; teacher helping more. 4 pupils could give no particular reason.

The pupils (27%) whose feelings towards modern languages learning had become more negative gave a wider range of reasons, reflecting a response of a much more individual nature. 2 pupils simply said they felt generally negative. 5 pupils referred to a decline in interest during Year 8, and 5 said it now took a long time to learn a few things, or that little new was learnt, or that topics went on a long time. 5 commented that they found the work less interesting than in Year 7 (less speaking, less exciting, less stimulating). 4 mentioned their teacher (not liking the teacher, unable to understand the teacher, teachers not accepting that the pupil finds the work hard, the teacher constantly interrupting pupils' work). Other comments by individual pupils were: class too talkative; lost interest after first 3 or 4 lessons; own standard declined so dropped a set; too many tests; making better progress in other subjects.

2 pupils expressed a more ambivalent response, saying that their response to lessons was affected by the mood of the teacher, and by how much the teacher helped them with the problems they met that day.

The overall picture of these pupils' attitudes towards modern languages learning is complex. They are not, on this evidence, by any means all losing interest over time. There is little evidence of xenophobia or other restricted thinking. Many pupils sustain their level of interest well and are adding their sense of the importance of the subject to their enjoyment of it. But many pupils seem to express a sense of frustration: they are aware that language learning involves the development of higher-order skills and understanding which they glimpse from time to time but which seem to remain beyond their ability to master.

5 ▶ Summary of findings

This section summarises the content of Section 4, the pupils' responses.

Question group A: preference

Comparison with other subjects

Modern languages received an overall ranking of sixth out of seven when compared with six other selected subjects. They were given the lowest number of extreme rankings (i.e. favourite or least favourite subject). Gender difference was not significant.

Reasons for subject preference

In all seven subjects, pupil preference was based on classroom experience rather than any perception of a subject's importance. Active work, interest, enjoyment and variety were the main reasons for preference.

Question group B: modern language lessons

Perceptions of progress

Most pupils stated that they thought they were doing well or fairly well in their modern language work. They frequently quoted progress they felt they were making in the skills of speaking, reading and writing. They also mentioned positive feedback from teachers in the form of comments or marks and test results. Little reference was made to specific aspects of progression involving, for example, learning to handle or produce longer texts or greater complexity of language. Those pupils who stated that they were not doing well tended to perceive the subject as difficult in a general way, rather than referring to specific difficulties of which they were aware. Some indicated that learning a language is hard, others that they were simply not good at it.

Classroom activities

Pupils identified, from a list of 25 activities, what they do in their modern language lessons. A picture emerged of classrooms characterised by a fairly standard range of processes, e.g. working with a partner, working through the textbook, answering teacher's questions. Other activities, such as working with longer texts, listening to native speakers, working with video and using IT, were found only in a minority of lessons.

Pupils were asked to identify activities they liked or disliked, and activities they found particularly helpful or unhelpful. Little emerged by way of a clear shared view of the enjoyment and value they attribute to the activities that they  commonly do: pupils seem not to think about their language learning in these terms.

On video: 'You can pick up a lot while relaxing'.

Pupils did not appear to have a strong sense of liking or disliking the majority of the 25 listed activities, though there were more explicit statements of liking than of disliking. Gender difference was not significant. Given the efforts made to make language learning and resources as stimulating as possible, the degree of indifference must be of concern, especially since pupils explain their subject preferences in terms of the classroom experience.

Activities seen as particularly helpful included repeating what is heard, vocabulary tests and listening to tapes. Reasons for pupils' preferences were often imprecise, although some individual comments were mature and perceptive. Few of the more commonly done activities were described by pupils as unhelpful: the commonest examples here were copying, then drawing and labelling. Individual comments suggested that IT is not in itself useful or interesting if the activity is low-level.

> *In role play you 'act, express yourself, speak in a way you like best, have fun'.*

A number of activities, including doing exercises, attracted few judgements as to either their helpfulness or unhelpfulness. Pupils accepted that activities they did not like might be helpful.

Awareness of learning objectives

Pupils experienced great difficulty when asked to reflect, even in simple terms, on the learning objectives of their most recent lesson. Their attempts to talk about the work were often unclear and inarticulate. Many references were made to activities, but there was little evidence that pupils had seen their purpose in terms of bringing about learning.

Awareness of learning

Notwithstanding the above, the great majority of pupils then went on to say that they had succeeded, to a greater or lesser extent, in achieving the learning objectives of their last lesson. However, few were able to give any direct evidence as to precisely what had been learnt. Judgements tended to be based on successfully completing activities or tasks rather than on the development of knowledge, skills or understanding.

Landmarks of achievement

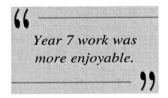

> *Year 7 work was more enjoyable.*

About a quarter of the pupils claimed to be able to quote an aspect of real linguistic achievement which had occurred during the last three years and of which they were proud, such as making up a poem. Only one pupil referred to a point of linguistic understanding (French definite articles). Others referred to broader areas, such as events or activity types, rather than individual achievements. Few 'landmarks' related to Year 9. 13 pupils could not recall anything that they had achieved of particular merit.

Question group C: language learning

Factors leading to success

When asked to suggest factors associated with successful language learning, pupils mentioned general study skills, positive attitudes and overall linguistic aptitude as well as language-specific skills. Pronunciation was seen by some almost as an innate ability, rather than as a skill that can be taught and learnt.

Problems

> *If you learn how to pronounce words it should help you.*

When pupils talked about the problems they encountered, it became clear that many were not yet getting past the obstacles of the sound, meaning and spelling of individual words. Little evidence was seen of pupils having the confidence or skills to acquire language through exposure to its everyday use in the classroom and the textbook. Some tried, though with limited success, to articulate problems relating to grammar.

Sources of help

Most pupils said that they usually got enough help when they met problems. The teacher was quoted as the prime source, although partners and reference materials were also mentioned by many. On closer investigation, it emerged that the help received is usually of a type designed to help with completion of the task in hand, rather than of a type which provides pupils with the skills to cope with similar difficulties in the future.

Organisation of work

Most pupils mentioned doing their writing in exercise books on a page-by-page basis. Exercises, copied work, notes and vocabulary are thus recorded in chronological sequence as they go. The use of separate vocabulary books is not widespread. There were many small exceptions and variations to this pattern, even within individual schools. The general picture is one of a lack of organisation of pupils' work.

Most pupils said that they could find all, or some, of their old exercise books. These books were referred to mainly for topic revision rather than as reference materials for points of structure or grammar, though some pupils mentioned an interest in seeing how they have moved on from their earlier work.

Textbooks

All pupils said that they used a textbook in lessons and over half said that they had their own book at all times. When asked to explain how the textbook was helpful, pupils most often referred to word lists and glossaries, followed by end-of-unit revision sections. Pupils did not refer to their textbooks as interesting, stimulating or enjoyable.

Question group D: progress

Higher standards

Most pupils felt that the standard of their work had risen over the three years in which they had been learning their foreign language. The nature of this progress was expressed variously. Some spoke of their own general sense of improvement, others mentioned only confirmation from others. Examples given included: knowing more words, having longer conversations, better marks and test results attained. Again, no clear and agreed view emerged.

Teaching for improvement

Pupils described what teachers do to help them improve. Mention was made of more demanding work and general motivational factors such as encouragement. Pupils also spoke of clear instructions, explanations and individual support. Little mention was made of teachers giving pupils specific skills and techniques to enable them to handle these problems successfully in future (see note on 'sources of help', p53).

Question group E: attitudes

Importance of foreign language learning

About 75% of the pupils stated positively that language learning was important. The reasons most commonly quoted related to job prospects and qualifications, although visits and holidays also featured. Those with direct or indirect foreign connections were more likely to say that languages are important.

Pupils' views of parental attitudes

Most pupils said that their parents were positive about their children learning a foreign language. Almost a quarter of pupils referred to the family as providing a context and/or specific support for their language learning.

Gender and aptitude

When asked if girls are better at language learning than boys (or vice-versa), 71% of pupils said there were no differences, with one pupil unsure. Just over a quarter thought that girls were better, giving reasons that related mainly to matters of attitude and behaviour. No pupil thought that boys were better than girls.

First experience of foreign language learning

When asked to recall their reactions to their first foreign language lesson, pupils' responses were generally clear and positive. Apprehension and nervousness were quickly dispelled. Very few pupils had an abiding negative memory.

Current experience of foreign language learning

35% of pupils said they felt more positive towards language learning now than when they started in Year 7. Confidence, a sense of progress and an awareness of the importance of the language were important factors to these pupils: these are all aspects of extrinsic motivation. 37% said their feelings (whether positive or negative) had not changed with time. 27% now felt less positive about language learning than when they started. These pupils provided a wide range of reasons for their views, including a lack of interest and variety, a sense that they were making little progress, and poor relationships with the teacher. All these are issues of intrinsic motivation; they are not counterbalanced by any extrinsic factors in the case of these pupils.

Section

6 ▶ Discussion of findings
Jeff Lee

In this section there are frequent references to 'a learner' or 'an individual'. In this connection masculine pronouns and possessive adjectives are used, simply to avoid making the text unwieldy with constant references to 'he or she' and 'him or her'.

This research project was based in a specific local context and carried out with 62 specific pupils. Any conclusions can in the first instance apply only to that context and those pupils. Whether they can be applied more generally will depend on how representative the local context and the pupils are judged to be. The project team hopes nonetheless that the following view of the possible implications for modern languages curriculum and pedagogy will be of interest to teachers of modern languages and also to those involved with school management and with modern language curriculum design and policy, both at local and national level.

The overall picture

We are dealing here with pupils of average ability, pupils who do not show particular aptitude in that they do not learn especially quickly. Nor, however, do they have particular or special learning difficulties. Nor do they, on this showing, take the line that learning a language is irrelevant to them; they accept languages as much as they accept any other part of the school curriculum. This may not apply to similar pupils everywhere, but it is argued that boosting the intrinsic motivation levels of pupils is the key to sustaining their interest. Motivation will play a vital role in making them willing to persevere with their language learning, both in the short and long term. Leaving aside the small percentage of pupils who by accident of birth or genes have a natural advantage for language learning, the great majority of language learners will succeed to the extent that they make best use of the time and teaching available to them. The average pupil needs help in all this, but the crucial factor will be the extent to which they understand the nature and purpose of what they are being asked to do and believe that effort makes a difference to their performance.

It is possible to sketch an overall picture, in simple terms, of the pupils' experiences, their responses to them, and the progress they feel they are making. The pupils were without exception responsive in the interviews and pleased to be selected to take part in them: the self-esteem of many grew during the process. They talked about their modern language learning in mainly neutral or positive terms. Very little came through as explicitly negative, although in overall preference terms modern languages rated low against other subjects. Only one or two indicated that they thought learning a language was pointless. Clearly pupils think their teachers do much to help them learn. Teachers have succeeded in persuading them of the importance of learning a foreign language, especially in terms of future employment. Pupils rely heavily on their teachers and place great trust in them.

On the down side, the pupils have a limited view of the nature and process of learning a foreign language. This emerges through their inability to talk, in anything other than vague terms, about what they are intended to learn, what has been learnt, and the extent to which they are successful in their learning, based on clear evidence and an understanding of what is going on. They talk broadly about what they have done in lessons. They describe in Year 9 a similar experience and approach to that found in Year 7, but without some of the attractions or the novelty value. Textbooks, video and IT are making little impact. They characterise lessons in terms of activities and topics. Although a few pupils mention producing longer sentences, most make no reference to what might be called real linguistic progression in terms of handling longer texts, or producing more complex language, or for example being able to talk about things that happened in the past. The same might well apply, in equivalent terms, to other subject areas, but if so it is perhaps a point of more general concern that pupils aged thirteen to fourteen should have such a limited view of their learning.

The detail of what these pupils say can be examined at length. But the most prominent messages emerging seem to be that the pupils, for all their 'invisibility', are interested in their education and in talking sensibly and at some length about one aspect of it. They have plenty to say, and what they say is often illuminating, but they are not well equipped readily to articulate it. They derive some enjoyment and a sense of progress from their work, but the value of much of what they do escapes them. They do not seem to know why they are learning or doing particular things. Some of them imply that they are aware of things going on behind their work which they cannot grasp. They may unwittingly be describing the effect on them of representative current approaches to modern language teaching, with its emphasis on chunks of language met in the context of a topic.

On this basis, the position is certainly not one of profound dissatisfaction or total demotivation on the part of the pupils. On the contrary, many say it is important to know a modern foreign language. But there is scope for raising the level of their motivation, in particular the intrinsic aspects, and for ensuring they develop positive views of the social and cultural advantages. Their standards of attainment could be raised likewise. It is argued that suitable starting points and directions for this work can be more easily found by listening carefully to what they say, as in this research. What they say suggests that they are not well prepared for work in Key Stage 4 and beyond, with its increasing demands on them in terms of knowledge, skills, and understanding. Their ability to work independently will be constrained by the difficulties they describe at word level to do with sounds, spellings and meanings, and further by the problems they have in making combinations of words work for them 'in the way Sir does', as one pupil memorably put it. Pupils said that when they started learning a language there was some apprehension, but very few said they were negatively predisposed to the work. This report argues that pupils' motivation levels are not fixed: they can be influenced by the provision they receive and the experiences they undergo as a result.

Aspects of motivation

Motivation is not a readily measured attribute unless simplistic aspects are considered such as the time a learner is prepared to spend on a task. Nor is it a standard force or influence acting on all learners in the same way. On the contrary, individuals are motivated by different things depending on their personal attributes. Past research has explored various lines in this field. But there are a number of common features which apply in the great majority of situations and cases. These notes describe two general aspects which it might be helpful for teachers and others to bear in mind when they think about what kind of curriculum and teaching might best motivate the pupils for whom they are responsible.

A basic definition involves a distinction between **intrinsic** and **extrinsic** motivation: intrinsic motivation stemming from the individual's personal interest in the subject being learnt, extrinsic from external factors such as rewards, qualifications or job prospects. Both are important and powerful influences. In simple terms the first four question groups (A–D) were designed to extract information about intrinsic motivation; group E related more, though not exclusively, to extrinsic motivation.

The pupils in the project – and, according to pupils, most of their parents — are persuaded of the importance of learning a language for purposes of employment or possible future travel and contacts: extrinsic motivation is quite high. But the answers and reasons given for pupils' subject preferences in Questions 1 and 2 were based very firmly not on the possible value of a subject for later life, but on their experiences of it at classroom level: in other words, the intrinsic interest and appeal of the work was what determined their choices.

Gender-related issues

This research found relatively few differences between boys and girls in overall terms. The 31 boys and 31 girls in the project perceive differences — with a fair degree of accuracy — not so much in terms of innate facility as in the way they respond to lessons: in other words it could be that girls do better at languages than boys simply because they spend more of the time available actually focusing on the work they are given to do. This would support a view of aptitude as closely related to the time needed for and spent on learning. One interpretation of this could be that girls are more willing to try to understand and follow the instructions they are given, while boys may be less inclined to do so.

The current project deals only with how pupils perceive such differences in modern language learning, not whether their views are correct, justified, or confirmed by other observers. Most see no or little difference, but a significant number are beginning to collect, at age fourteen, some intimation of what tends to emerge at GCSE and generally in terms of girls' superior academic performance. Other issues which might arise from further investigation would be pupils' responses to female as opposed to male teachers (including the issue of voice and intonation models) and pupils' perceptions of gender differences in other subjects. Also on the gender issue, there is the question of teachers' perceptions of boys and girls in the classroom, and whether male and female teachers interact differently with them.

Principles for enhancing motivation levels in modern language learning

One of the starting points for the project was the issue of how to make average ability pupils better motivated to learn a foreign language. This can be expressed as a set of linked questions:

- What are the factors most likely to make pupils of average ability want to work hard and persevere at learning a language?

- Are they mainly points of belief, attitude or personality, or are there also factors relating to the provision and experiences they receive?

- To what extent are these different factors controllable by teachers and pupils? Can pupils be helped to a higher level of motivation, and if so how?

- What can and should be done to promote positive beliefs and attitudes on the part of as many pupils as possible?

- What kind of curriculum will help to bring this about?

- What kind of teaching will help to bring it about?

Some answers to the above questions can be tentatively offered on the basis of this project and other research, in the form of a set of suggested principles for maximising motivation levels in the learning of modern languages. These are set out here in a collective form and in terms of positive and negative factors: things to be brought about, and things to be avoided.

It should be borne in mind that the focus here is on actual classroom practice, the day-to-day work with which teachers and pupils are regularly involved. The emphasis is also on enhancing intrinsic rather than extrinsic motivation, by looking for those factors which engage the learners most directly and personally with the learning. Additional provision such as visits abroad, cultural contacts, and one-off activities such as French or German days are invaluable because they provide an opportunity for pupils to prove to themselves and others that they can use the language they have learnt, but they are by definition the exception rather than the rule.

Suggested principles for maximising motivation

Pupils need to have or to experience:

- a sense of achievement and a belief that they can improve — the 'I can do it' feeling;
- a realisation that this stems from their own efforts rather than from random external factors;
- a sense of curiosity about the language they are learning — a desire to see what is happening underneath;
- a clear understanding of what learning a language is about, including the terminology involved, and of how they can know when they are making progress in it;
- the realisation that they are developing skills of language use and language learning and acquiring techniques of mastering new language and applying it in new situations;
- goals set for them which are at a moderate level — challenging but achievable;
- helpful learning activities which are clearly not assessment tasks;
- feedback which helps and shows them how to improve as well as indicating their standard;
- active involvement in the work of the lesson;
- a sense, in an appropriate way, of control over their work and progress.

They should not develop or receive:

- a belief that their personal efforts will have no effect on their standard and progress;
- a belief that aptitude for learning a language is something fixed and owned by others, rather than an issue of time needed for learning;
- a high level of test anxiety born of a fear that they are always being assessed;
- confusion over the nature and purpose of what they are doing, both over time and in individual lessons;
- high praise for doing an easy task with little effort;
- an excessive emphasis on extrinsic sources of motivation;
- lessons which involve them in long periods of passive working.

Suggestions for the curriculum and teaching

It is not the purpose of this report to set out in detail a programme of teaching and provision which will neatly address all the issues arising from this project. Motivation is too complex and too personal. It is for teachers and curriculum planners to consider whether the findings apply generally or in particular cases. In terms of current practice, one issue which arises at once is that of target language use. Giving pupils a clearer view of the objectives behind the curriculum and lessons has to be reconciled somehow with the central place of the target language in current methodology. As a starting point, pupils should be helped at least to indicate that they have a problem and ask for help through the medium of the foreign language. However, it may well be easier for teachers of other subjects, obviously working in English, to gauge the motivational levels of pupils and, more importantly, give them long-term help by talking with them, or by listening to what they say about their experiences. On the other hand, exactly the same problem might apply in that there is commonly insufficient time for in-depth discussion with individual pupils. However, this research suggests that if quality time can be found in this way and pupils helped to overcome their long-term difficulties, certainly at Key Stage 3, it can provide invaluable guidance for schools and teachers and is in itself a motivating experience for pupils.

That said, the following notes are presented to suggest how the development of modern language teaching might respond to the key questions raised in this research and how the criteria set out above for enhancing motivation levels might be taken further.

- The modern languages curriculum and the related learning experiences need to be made much more transparent, so that pupils of average ability especially are able to see much more clearly the purposes behind what they are doing, both in lessons and over time.

- The teaching should include clear and precisely specified learning intentions. The objectives commonly given to pupils at the start of typical textbook units are totally inadequate. Learning intentions must identify the specific language content of the unit, what aspects of this content are to be learnt (e.g. sound/meaning/spelling), what skills are to be taught (both use of language and language learning skills), and what understanding of language operations and functions is to be mastered by pupils. These learning intentions must be made clear in an appropriate and meaningful way to pupils, especially in the case of those of average ability and below who are not confident working deductively without such guidance. The issue of how to reconcile this requirement with the principle of target language use will need to be addressed.

- Some aspects of currently accepted practice in foreign language teaching need to be questioned in the light of the need for a clearer view of pedagogical issues and an appropriate methodology.

- Pupils need appropriate time to master the various aspects of language learning. This time needs to be generated by reviewing the value, in terms of pupil progress and learning, of activities commonly done and the time devoted to them. Examples quoted by pupils are excessive copying and drawing/labelling. These pupils need more direct and focused help to move from the presentation phase to the application/manipulation phase. The 'chunk' approach must be modified as these pupils move into the middle stages of language learning.

- The skills of language acquisition must be fixed in learners early if they are to develop independence later. This includes the understanding of principles which will help them in long-term learning, as opposed to resolving simply the immediate problem with a word. They need to be taught, for example, patterns and techniques in pronunciation; they need to be helped to see patterns in grammar, so that they can make sense of what is going on behind the words they see written down or hear being used.

- A consensus is needed on the most common items of terminology used in foreign language teaching. The meanings of terms such as knowledge, skills and understanding need to be clearly defined and used consistently. Activities and tasks should be seen as different in nature and purpose, with activities being used for teaching, practice and reinforcement, whereas tasks are fundamentally assessment operations.

- Pupils can and must be taught how to memorise new language items in terms which are clear to them. Techniques for helping them to do so are fairly well known, especially where the vocabulary is, for example, a list of clothing items or school subjects: in other words vocabulary related closely to specific topics.

- However, pupils have problems usually at a different level, to do with the smaller words and features of a language which do not naturally arise in or belong to any topic but are found all over the place: pronouns, verbs, small items such as 'c'est' in French, everyday adverbs or conjunctions, everyday interrogative words, the difference between '*je*' and '*j'ai*'; indeed almost any language items other than lists of homogeneous, topic-based vocabulary. They need to be shown how these items work since without them pupils do indeed stay at the word list level, or the level of their basic chunks. This approach could be an intermediate stage to help pupils manipulate the language they know as memorised chunks, but preceding any detailed work on specific points of grammar.

- Pupils need to be shown what constitutes a quality response at any level. Teachers should be able to offer pupils a model of a good response to any given task, so that they know what they have to emulate. They then need to be taught to emulate it. (This is not the same as an example in an exercise or task, or a sample of authentic foreign language in a textbook: these are again based on the assumption that pupils will be able to work deductively from them, which relatively few can do without further guidance.)

- Pupils need to be taught the precise techniques which they need in order to incorporate, for example, a new language item into known language. Teachers need to show pupils explicitly and repeatedly, as a class, how this is done, and get pupils to emulate and demonstrate this process repeatedly and accurately as a basis for independent work later.

- Pupils sometimes need help with and demonstration of basic routines such as how to set out their work, note new language items, etc. Their pride in their written and earlier work would in this way be increased.

- Curriculum, teaching and course materials need to take all the above into account. Most course books are far too vague in the way they specify learning objectives, for example. Teachers need to know **in precise terms** the purpose of a given set of materials, how such materials are to be used and the learning that is supposed to accrue from their use.

Final comments

Many other questions could have been put to the pupils, or could be at a later stage on the basis of their answers here. It may be useful to carry out further research on, for example, effective memorising, pair work, note-taking, or the teaching of language application techniques. At some stage it might be valuable to go back to the pupils interviewed in this project, or indeed work with them on the problems they have identified. It is hoped that discussions with textbook publishers, researchers, curriculum and course designers might ensue and further inform developments in modern language teaching and learning. The pupils who so willingly gave us their time and shared their thoughts and their feelings with us deserve nothing less. Nor do the teachers who work with such commitment and who have persuaded their pupils of the essential place of modern languages in their education.

Appendix

The interview questions

─────────── ◀▶ ───────────

A: PREFERENCE

1   Put these subjects in order of preference (using cards): mathematics,
    English, French or German (as applied in individual cases), science,
    geography, history, technology.
    (Ask individually)

2   Why do you prefer the subject you've put as no. 1?
    (Ask individually)

B: MFL LESSONS

3   Do you think that you are doing well in (Fr/Ge)? Why (not)?
    (Ask individually)

    *N.B. answers to Questions 4, 5, 6, 7 and 8 were entered as ticks on a
    grid, set out below. Pupils' additional comments on Questions 7 and 8
    were noted separately.*

4   What kind of things do you do in your (Fr/Ge) lessons?
    (Ask as a pair; tick from list, q.v.)

5   Which activities do you particularly like doing?
    (Ask individually)

6   Which activities do you dislike doing?
    (Ask individually)

7   Which of these activities help you to learn better? How?
    (Ask individually)

8   Which of these activities do not help you to learn better? Explain.
    (Ask individually)

Answer grid for Questions 4–8

Language learning activities	do	like	dislike	help	not help
answering the teacher's questions					
repeating what you hear					
copying from the board or from a book					
listening to the teacher explain things					
working through the textbook					
listening to a tape					
listening to a native speaker of the foreign language in person					
drawing and labelling					
doing exercises, e.g. gap filling, true/false, matching things					
vocabulary tests					
reading short passages					
reading longer passages — more than a page					
working things out, e.g. how words sound, why some words have different endings					
being creative, e.g. making up a conversation, writing something of your own					
acting — role play					
reading aloud					
giving a spoken presentation to the class					
playing games					
singing					
using computers					
using dictionaries					
using video					
learning about the foreign country					
working with a partner					
working in groups					

9   Think back to your last lesson. Were you clear what you were supposed to learn from it?
    (Ask individually. Push towards 'learn', rather than 'do'.)

10 If answer to 9 is 'Yes': Did you succeed? How do you know?
    If answer is 'No': What did you learn?
    (Ask individually. Push towards 'learn', rather than 'do'.)

11 What is the best thing you have achieved in your (Fr/Ge) work so far?
    (Ask individually)

C: LANGUAGE LEARNING

12 What do you need in order to learn a language well? Suggested prompt: For instance, you may need to have a good memory. What other skills might you need?
    (Ask as a pair)

13 What sort of problems do you come across when you are trying to learn?
    (Ask as a pair)

14 When you have a problem, do you usually get enough help of the sort you need?
    (Ask as a pair)

15 Where do you get help?
    (Ask as a pair)

Incidental questions

16 How do you organise your work — books, folders, etc.?
    Ask if necessary:
    • do you have places for recording vocabulary, grammar?
      (ask as a pair)
    • could you find all your old exercise books/folders if asked?
      (ask individually)
    • do you ever use your old exercise books/folders? If so, how?
      (ask individually)

17 Do you use a textbook in lessons?
    Is it helpful? How?
    (Ask as a pair)

18 Do you have your own textbook?
    (Ask as a pair)

D: PROGRESS

19 You have been learning (Fr/Ge) for nearly three years now. Do you
    think that the standard of your work is getting higher?
    If answer is 'Yes': In what way?
    Possible prompt: For instance, you may be expected to speak for
    longer or to write more words on a topic about yourself.
    (Ask as a pair)

20 How does your teacher help you to raise the standard of your work?
    (Ask as a pair — refer back to points made on previous question)

E: ATTITUDES

21 Do you think it is important to learn a foreign language?
    (Ask individually)

22 What do your parents think about your learning a foreign language?
    (Ask individually)

23 Do you think (girls) are better at language learning than (boys)?
    (Ask question both ways round) Explain.
    (Ask as a pair)

24 How did you feel about your first ever foreign language lesson?
    (Ask individually)

25 Have your feelings changed?
    If yes: (a) in what way? (b) why?
    (Ask individually)